T0113588

Short and Simple

Order this book online at www.trafford.com
or email orders@trafford.com

Most Trafford titles are also available at major online book retailers.

Print information available on the last page.

ISBN: 978-1-6987-0791-4 (sc)
ISBN: 978-1-6987-0793-8 (hc)
ISBN: 978-1-6987-0792-1 (e)

Library of Congress Control Number: 2021912145

Trafford rev. 06/23/2021

Trafford
PUBLISHING®   www.trafford.com
North America & international
toll-free: 844-688-6899 (USA & Canada)
fax: 812 355 4082

Like the dialogue of a teenage girl.
An abundance of subtext,
A shortage of words.

To my younger self for choosing to
believe in herself as much as she
believed in fairies.
She paved the way for me, and I am
paving the way for my higher self.

They asked me how my day was.
I said "Ok."
They didn't pry out the truth
Because my mood to them was a teenage cliché.

I don't want my parents to treat me like a baby and
hold my hand
Like they used to when they walked me to
fairyland.
But my hand forgot what it was like having
company.
It's like you want to be isolated and then
suddenly…
You just want to be cradled by somebody.

I can't let you write the story of your life
Where both the protagonist and antagonist are
written as you
You pulled the knife
But you also felt the pain seep through

How many times can we say the overused lie of
"I'm fine"
For someone in society to look us in the eyes
And accept that it is human to feel, and that it's
human to cry

Slamming the door to my room doesn't necessarily mean I don't want to talk to my parents. Sometimes it's a hidden invitation for them to walk in.

Everyone's eyes are on the teenage girl.
How is she dressing?
How does she look?
Does she have an attitude?
Is she really an open book?
Is it that time of the month?
How much is she eating at lunch?
Does she start drama?
Do her friends?
Is she invited to plans?
Or does it depend?

Everyone's eyes are on the teenage girl.
Be careful how you treat her.
You are influencing her beliefs in this world.

One day I am so scared of being weird.
The next day I tell myself I should own my weirdness.
One day I resent the girls who are considered cool.
The next day I wonder what's in the mind of those who appear to be fearless.

Observe how girls treat girls.
Some are out there sharpening their words, like they
would a knife.

You think the weather is unstable…
Observe a friend group of girls.

I want to start a petition to end the use of the word
"popular"
The word that takes a diamond and calls it a
commoner
Social hierarchy is intoxicating innocent minds
It's shocking to see that adults too feed into these
crimes

I think one of weirdest feelings is the feeling of not
knowing what you're feeling.
You're just a teenager with your head leaning
against the wall.
Not crying, not feeling dumb
Not smiling, not feeling numb

What does it feel like to feel?
It's realizing there is a river inside each of us that
has been blocked off by the wall of our skin.
It's becoming a magician and pulling the endless
string of the feelings we bury within.
It's feeling the rapids pour from our soul, to our
heart, to our swollen and spent eyes
To dissecting irrational thoughts, figuring out which
are truths and which are lies.

It's funny, because when I really *feel*, I can't
describe how I feel at all.
Because when I pour I'm not sad.
I'm not bitter.
I'm not mad.
I'm just a girl in pain.
I'm just a girl who has become one with the rain.
Though the men in my life like to blame my moods
on my period,
They don't understand that women are warriors and
to break, it takes something far more serious.
I'm just a girl crying alone in the kitchen.
I'm the voice that gets swallowed by other voices,
so everything I have to say is written.

When I was little I was free
I wasn't scared or ashamed to show off me
I used to model on the runway I made out of pool
towels
This was when I was still learning the difference
between consonants and vowels
Now I'm at that age
Where girls lock up their authentic self in a cage
I just wonder when we'll take out the keys
And decide it's time for the world to see
Who we are once we allow ourselves to be

I hate when older people tell us that work is work
and it doesn't have to be enjoyable.
They are programming us with the belief
That what we dedicate our time to doesn't have to
make us feel complete.

I'm sorry I didn't call you.
I know you are mad at me for that.
But you didn't call me either.
I was waiting for you to initiate for *once*.
And *I* was mad at *you* for that.

We are all so scared of others running away
That we forgot the most natural form of leaving is
drifting away

You're not running
You're drifting
Drifting away
And that's why it hurts

That's why it hurts.

If someone in your life secretly decides to rent a
boat and sail away
Maybe it's not because they're drifting away from
you
But because they were just drifting away from
themselves

Sometimes I feel like the mirror is the only shoulder available when I cry.

What is the story you are telling yourself as to why
you can't achieve your dreams *right* now?
Commit to the journey, don't commit to the how.

I never considered myself as somebody who has
anxiety
But then I feel my heart doing jumping jacks
Whenever I have to speak, stand, or walk in front of
people.
Especially in front of those who remind me of those
who hurt me.

"For some reason I have always valued chosen
family
When my chosen family hasn't chosen me"

-Me a few months ago

"I haven't chosen myself first. That's the reason"

-Me now

When I close my eyes and envision a version of
myself 10 years in the future
My shoulders look so light and
I can't wait to align with myself

Why is it so hard for me to surrender to the idea that
happiness is something possible for me to attain?
It's very possible that I am my own drain
I've only been accepting the rain
Neglecting the fact that the sun and I were born to
shine the same

When lunch stops becoming your favorite period of the day, and the most dreaded one
The universe is poking your arm telling you to wake up and start the journey of self discovery.
You need to find yourself, and through that you will find your people.

When your mind gets wrapped up in the clouds,
even the most simple tasks
such as tying your shoe
become impossible.
The laces keep slipping from your fingers and you
just can't tie the simple knot.

Like a fish in a tank
You provide it with food
You provide it with water
You give it a shelter
When its home is the ocean

To choose to hear the words
While choosing to ignore the tone
Says that you're either oblivious
Or find it easiest to be ignorant

I ask a lot of questions
Most of which I know the answers to
I'm just trying to start a conversation
I'm struggling to talk with this new unfamiliar you

We are all just combinations of the people we know.

Dear Boys,

We are not just something you could "tap"

Sincerely,
Women

When I say "leave me alone"
I mean "I need you to stay and pry my feelings out
of me because I feel uncomfortable and
embarrassed expressing them to you when you
didn't ask for that and I am going through so much
and I'm so lonely and I just need you to hug me
please don't go and take my harsh words and tone
personally I'm just trying to get you to want to get
to the bottom of what's happening with my
emotions because I need to talk it out."

Someday I'll look at somebody and see my second home.
Because my first home is myself.

As little girls we are told
"Don't let anyone treat you like anything less than a
princess"
That one day we would find our prince.
But people often forget to tell us to treat ourselves
like princesses.
I believe that should come first
As it determines what kind of prince we think we
are worthy of.

I don't care that fairytales are unrealistic
I will create the most fantastical vision of the future
And create my own fairytale
Laugh all you want
But I won't be there to hear you
Because I'll be gone
Living my own happily ever after

If I am the princess
My thoughts are the peas
Keeping me awake
Feeding me irrational stories

I can't continue being a sponge
Absorbing everyone else's crap
And relying on someone else to wring it out

Halloween can be scary for a teenage girl.
Not for the decorations
Not for the movies
Not for the horror stories
But for the concept of choosing a costume.

For some,
Halloween is everyday.

Haha, I just remembered I used to climb trees and derive love from all the little things. I used to marvel at the fuzzy caterpillar that I wondered was poisonous and watched it inch up the tree.

In second grade we learn about the weather.
When my mom drove me home from school I
would look at the cumulonimbus clouds I just
learned about and smile.
I told her it was going to rain.
It did.
I thought I was going to be a f***ing meteorologist
prodigy

When parents ask "how was school?"
And we answer "It was fine" without any extra
details,
We really mean that there is pain in our heart
From feeling dumb,
Feeling lonely,
Or feeling ostracized

I have denied having an eating disorder
But doing jumping jacks in the middle school
bathroom says otherwise
and
Enjoying hearing "you look like a skeleton" says
otherwise

Denying a problem doesn't stop it from becoming
real
Denying a problem delays you from beginning to
heal

If you are telling yourself that exercise is fun
While telling your body that it is unworthy
Then I want to tell you
That your body works beautiful miracles for you
You are a beautiful miracle
Yes you are.
You are.

Young artists,

Adults may tell you that your art seems too dark.
They might even criticize you and talk down to you
about your work.
What they fail to remember is that our art is what
saves us.
Our art is a healthy outlet for self expression.
Without our art, we are like the adults that talk
down to us.
People who suppress their emotions, rather than
express them.

I tailored myself to fit the standard.
I tailored myself like a thread and needle would a
pair of pants.
I cut off the parts of me that seemed like "too
much"
To now realize that those parts are the parts that
make me
And those parts are more than enough.

If our destinies are written in the stars
What a shame we struggle deciphering the
handwriting

You are waiting for your miracle
While your miracle has been waiting for you too.
You are looking in the external world
When your miracle originated inside of you.
Your miracles always have and always will be
created within.
But you will miss them if you're too busy pulling
apart your own skin.

My ambition is negated by my self sabotage
I crave to be different, but I'm hiding in camouflage

The transition from magical child to tired teen goes
like this:
No more hide and seek with our friends, but hide
and seek with society.

Stages of life coincide with stages of thought

I'm walking on a tightrope
On the other side are all of my friends
The rope is thinning
I'm beginning
To feel the only connection is on my end

High quality thoughts, high quality life.
Low quality thoughts, low quality life.

My mind and my heart are oil and water
Love attempts to be present but my mind is stronger
The heart's eyes are on the prize but the mind's
doubt remains a wanderer.

My heart brushes through my mind's knotted hair
Attempting to uncondition the mind from cowering
when society stares
The heart, a natural model with its confident strides
It's the mind who's a saunterer, it's the mind who
hides

My heart is sleeping on the potential of joy
With the mind tucking it in
Pounding on its hand of cards
While the heart sees potential for gin

A father cannot tell his daughter that there is no
such thing as the objectification of women
If he is also telling her to wear that extra layer
before she goes outside

What if these "failures" I'm facing are stepping
stones
that are guiding me to the big win

Stop teaching girls that boys hurt them because they
"mature slower than girls"
Maybe they mature slower because society allows
boys to get away with immature behavior while
girls are expected to grow up,
therefore they do

The quiet ones are deceiving
The quiet ones are internally screaming

The listener in your friend group
Needs a listener

I want to see the other side of your face
Because I see you when you say you are running a
solitary race
Advancing with toilsome strides towards a peaceful
headspace
My shoulder is yours
The haven where you can lay all your mind's floors
You don't have to speak for the world to hear your
roar
You don't have to fight alone to win this internal
war

Kids are growing up confusing real life from life
made by technology
This makes me laugh, because the scary reality of
this is so far from comedy

People say we're hormonal
People say we're in a phase
People say we're overemotional
People say we're living through all of the clichés

What else do you want to tell us that we are?
If we're feeling this way it's not because of
fabricated pain
It's because of emotional scars
Striving towards standards impossible to attain
Society's to blame

Don't tell me I'm not happy because my writing is
too deep
Would you prefer I adapt to your ways of putting
your emotions to sleep?
Or should I let them flow honestly?
Because honestly
I feel like you're asking me to live through your
approved set of lies
You're telling what's left of my childlike
authenticity to normalize

Why degrade yourself to being a candle
When you have the potential to be a raging fire
It takes only one person's breath to blow out a
candle
While no one can solely or collectively blow out a
fire.

I want you to open for me the cabinets in your mind
Let me see the silverware you use to eat
The self doubt you always seem to find

Tell me how you hold your head up that high
When your shoulders are turning in
And your soul is nudging you to cry

I want to go home
I want to surf above my emotional waves
Not get swallowed up
Not to have others say I'm in a phase

I dare you to smile at yourself in the mirror.

Do you see how beautiful you are?

Take another look.

You're a star

!

I'm tired of saying "When I grow up, I will..."
Because every single second of the day I am
evolving
The way I choose to spend every single second of
my day is determining what I will ....when I grow
up.
I'm growing up now.
And I will do everything I can within the seconds I
have to take care of the seeds I plant so one day
there will be flowers.

Every person has their own alphabet of expressions.

Right now while I feel like I'm swimming in
nothing
I somehow know that someday I will have
everything

Nothing is a gift!
It motivates you to create something
That means everything

You only "grow up" when you realize how much
more growing you need to do

Are all the grown ups you know grown up?

I'm tired of being in the background of everyone
else's picture
Poorer in love when there's a fire in me burning to
be richer

When did adults around us stop submerging us in magic and start submerging us in a world that wants to take our magic away?

If you consider yourself a "man," then don't only respect women when it comes to respecting your girlfriend.

They are telling us that our bodies are weaving in
and out of trend
They are serving us with a broken image we must
repeatedly mend
Telling us we're worthy depending on the day
Telling us we're worthy if we look the man's ideal
way

Why is it that when we correct boys' sexist jokes
we are deemed "radical?"

Repressing who you are
Is the most selfish act you could do
Depriving the world of your heart
People are burning for someone like you to relate to

We are playing peek-a-boo with society
Showing up
Hiding
Showing up
Hiding
Showing up
Hiding

I am embracing the fact that I am my own haven
If parts of me have gone astray, I can't rely on
others to save them

If I stop gripping on to what wishes to leave
My hands would be free
Available to reach for what's destined for me

Mom and Dad,

I don't want a reprimand. All I really need is for you to look me in the eyes and say that you *understand*.

My heart falls every time I step into math class
The concepts fall through my fingers like sand that
won't let itself be grasped
The sine function drives a dagger into my heart
Because it takes my brain with it through its ups and
downs convincing me I'm not smart

Test grades can't capture just how brilliant you are.
The number on the top right corner of your paper
Can't take away your ambition to make it far.
Can't take away your blessed hand of cards.
Can't take away your drive to strive past the "hard."

I've been my own best friend for the wrong reasons. While I was alone, I didn't have to fear judgment from others; I didn't have to fear talking too much, or too little; I didn't have to question whether or not people were laughing with me, or at me; I didn't have to fear looking the part; I didn't have to fear coming off as too stupid, or too "deep."

The real essence of life is lived through feeling all of your emotions.

I marched into the woods with pots and pans on my
head to hunt for fairies
In case they were to throw acorns at me,
It didn't phase me that I was marching through the
imaginary
Because when you believe in something so strongly
it becomes real
When you examine your beliefs you begin to heal

Preserve the magic inside of us we naturally had as
children
Let us keep our imagination because without it you
uncover holes we must later fill in
While I smiled at you with the natural love children
bear
You told me that life was a manmade series of
nightmares

It takes time to cry that the world is unfair.
It is.
But in that time you could have done what must be
done to repair it.

I was losing who I was
Before I even knew who I was

"I'd like to doodle the world with peace and grace
With united people joining hands
Speak only with kind words

I'd like to doodle the world with splatters of color
Paint children's faces with a smile
And make the world a little greener

I'd like to doodle the world with happiness and
dreams
To make beliefs and make your wishes come true
To follow your heart's desire and don't give up

I'd like to doodle the world with one more task
That's all I ask
Can you please help me
Doodle my heart's desire?"

-Written by 8 year old me

"Inside I start feeling insecure. That's just the beginning of losing confidence. Well I love acting, so I guess I can cover up how I feel."

-Written by 10 year old me

"My feelings are secretly boxed up in my heart and mind which feels like you are trapped and can't get out."

-Written by 10 year old me

The 8 year old me is wise beyond her years
The 10 year old me is swimming in all her fears
What happened between point A and point B?
I was filled with magic, then I let my magic drown
in society's man-made sea
That swallows up those who are late to conform to
"normalcy"

I am writing in collaboration with my younger self
She paved the way for me, and I am paving the way
for my higher self

While you're ashamed of your beauty
You unleash the beast
Invalidating the valid
Sabotaging your road to peace

Your journey is the evolution of your thoughts
Which control the evolution of your feelings

As children, we fall asleep to fairytales
As teens, we wake up to reality

I find more of who I am every time I connect my
thoughts to paper

The only thing you can trust is change. You are going to change. It's inevitable. But how you change...
That's all up to you.

It's your vision.

A complex, beautiful, unique vision.

They might not see it.

They might not believe it.

But they'll see it in fruition.

Because your entire being believed it was your duty; your mission.

...and the princess rescued herself, and she lived happily ever after. The end.

Printed in the United States
by Baker & Taylor Publisher Services